Table of Contents

Introduction

We see our soul in the flash of a knife,
Or atop a helmet.
And the autumn of salt
Spreads over our wounds
And in sight, there is no budding tree or spring.
-Syrian poet Adonis, from "Lamentations for Our Present Times"

Much of the Middle East has been in conflagration since unlicensed street vendor Mohamed Bouazizi set it alight on January 4, 2011. Tunisia's Ben Ali and Egypt's Mubarak were replaced by peaceful and popular revolt. Libya's Qadaffi went out with a minimum of Western military assistance and Yemen's president stepped down as well. Yet for nearly two years, the much more central Arab state of Syria has refuted overly-simplistic or optimistic analysis of the Arab Spring. There is no end in sight to the contest there between Bashar al-Asad's brutal but pluralist regime and its freedom-seeking but fundamentalist adversaries. At the end of 2012, the narrative of regional chaos and uncertainty has all but replaced 2011's narrative of a new birth of Arab freedom. Yet below these master-narratives lies the deeper question: What has changed? It is not simply, in the words of Pankaj Mishra, that "deep states can no longer bottle up political pressures created by globalized economies, modern communications and raised expectations."[1] This monograph argues that these political pressures themselves are the real story. In Tunisia and Egypt, Libya and Yemen, elections have brought Islamists into political power. In Syria, the opposition to Asad has a strongly Islamist component. Yet the very term "Islamist" must be parsed to understand its real significance.

The revival of the French Enlightenment term to describe the rise of political Islam, whether the AKP party in Turkey, the quondam Taliban government in Afghanistan, and the rise of the Muslim Brotherhood in the countries of the Arab Spring has been useful. The term seems to add a political form to a religious matter, or perhaps vice-versa, and has gained considerable acceptance. Nonetheless,

---

[1] Pankaj Mishra, "In 'Deep State' of Pakistan, an Unplanned Revolution Is Now Rewriting the Future," *The Jakarta Globe*, 24 April 2012, http://www.thejakartaglobe.com/opinion/in-deep-state-of-pakistan-an-unplanned-revolution-is-now-rewriting-the-future/513529 (accessed June 3, 2012).

1

something crucial is obscured by this term as well. Obscured is the fact that none of these phenomena are pan-Islamic. Rather, they are explicitly Sunni and often more than tacitly anti-Shia.

The Arab Spring ushers in a new paradigm of polarity for the region that is neither one of democracy vs. despotism, as Western idealists would like, even less of East vs. West as some Western realists fear. In its essence, it is neither an embrace nor a rejection of the West but a counter-reaction to the Shia Revival understood to have occurred since 2003. It is a Sunni Islamist Spring, i.e., a revival of a revanchist Sunni Islam eager to correct the perceived marginalization of Sunni Islam in recent history. It is not a new birth of political freedom for "The Arabs" as a political or ethnic whole. In sweeping away whatever lingered of a past paradigm of secular former regimes, the Arab Spring is the harbinger of a new religious and political identity that is explicitly Islamic, exclusively Sunni, and not limited to Arabs. Inherent in this Sunni counter-revival is a counter-reaction, to the perceived threat of a rising Shi'ism. It will move the Arab World away from its ethnic but minority-inclusive identification of Arab nationalism and Pan-Islamism and toward a greater unity with non-Arab Sunni powers. Being an explicitly Sunni phenomenon, it will heighten the divide in the Arab world between Sunni and Shia.

When Syrian President Bashar al-Asad falls to his Sunni Islamist opposition, the last outpost of secular pan-Arabism will fall with him. Paradoxically, Asad's fall will profoundly change the narrative that has grown in opposition to pan-Arabism as well, pan-Islamism. This is because Islam, as a religion and a polity, contains a bitter fault-line. Once Asad is no longer master of Syria, the internecine violence which experts believe will follow his departure will expand that fault line into a gulf that will tear open barely healed wounds in Iraq and Lebanon and rip new ones throughout the region. "I worry greatly that the minorities, the Alawis and the Christians, are going to be in for a very awful time," said retiring US Ambassador to Afghanistan Ryan Crocker, who added that "the repercussions for Syria, for Lebanon and Iraq, I think, can be pretty serious" if Sunni Islamists take over.[2] Order along the Sunni Islamist lines of

---

[2] Alissa J. Rubin, "Retiring U.S. Envoy to Afghanistan Exhorts Leaders to Heed Lessons of Past," *The New York Times*, 28 July 2012, http://www.nytimes.com/2012/07/29/world/asia/ambassador-crocker-sees-fraught-foreign-landscape-ahead.html?pagewanted=all (accessed August 15, 2012).

the emerging Arab world is, by its nature, unable to account for the aspirations of Shia Lebanon and Iraq, much less those of non-Arab Shias in Iran. It will certainly not account for the de facto Alawi and Christian state that may already be forming north of Lebanon along the Syrian coast. Rather, the political, economic and ethno-sectarian upheaval known as the Arab Spring could expand and institutionalize the divide between Sunni and Shia sub-civilizational blocs. The long-term result could culminate in a cleaving into distinct Sunni and Shia civilizations. Alternately, these countries could come to terms with a multi-polar Westphalian-style order of their own creation which respected sovereignty and fostered productive competition between its component states. It is also possible that the Middle East could come under the benign hegemony of a sufficiently inclusive and powerful state like Turkey that could restore a pan-Islamic unity and with it peace and prosperity. This monograph will weigh the likelihood and consider the implications of these possibilities. It will also consider the implications for American policy of the instability that lies along the path to any of these civilizational outcomes.

Methodology

As a complex socio-political phenomenon, the Arab Spring is not reducible to a single essentialist predication. It is not essentially or centrally about freedom, economics, politics, or religion, but a tapestry of continuities, trends and catalytic discontinuities such as a street vendor's despair or a poor wheat crop. Nonetheless, one particularly valuable master-narrative of the Middle East is its crisis of post-colonial identity. This crisis centers, according to David Fromkin, on the question of "how diverse peoples are to regroup to create new political identities for themselves after the collapse of an ages-old imperial order to which they had grown accustomed." Fromkin argues that the settlement of 1922, in which a post-Ottoman design for the region was proposed (or imposed) by the Allies, "is at the very heart of current wars, conflicts, and politics in the Middle East."[3] This may be the case but it must be qualified with the understanding that the reason the Ottoman break-up was so shattering has both a political and a religious

---

3 David Fromkin, *A Peace to End All Peace* (New York, NY: Henry Holt, 1989), 565.

3

dimension as did the Ottoman Empire. As such, it was a civilizational crisis and the Arab Spring is a continuation of this civilizational crisis.

To reconcile the rise of exclusivist Sunni Islamism in the Middle East and the marginalization of the region's pluralism with the notion that the Arab Spring is a sweeping away of prior attempts at transnational order, this monograph will plot the historical rise and fall of pan-Arabism and then the subsequent, and to a degree parallel, notion of pan-Islamism. By focusing on the modern history of these aspirational notions, the monograph will draw out of the historical detail a causal narrative that can account for the crisis of civilizational identity that the Arab Spring has unveiled. It will then follow this logic to a consideration of civilizational scenarios that could follow and the implications of each. First, though, let us establish the outlines of the frame of reference with which one may most productively view the Arab Spring.

Lenses to Discard

Some lenses are more useful than others in giving an accurate picture. Two hermeneutics cherished, respectively, by the two sides of the confrontationalist/accomodationist divide in American views on the rise of political Islam must be rejected at the outset.   Additionally, the notion that somehow the Arab Spring is America's beloved son born of our exertions in Iraq, a claim of some American and Middle East analysts and pundits, must be highly qualified.

In the first place, we must discard any heuristic that projects Western history or notions onto the events happening in the Middle East and views them in western terms. The most common example of this is to project the greatly oversimplified historical progression of renaissance-reformation-enlightenment-democracy as the path to modernity for Islam. In its simplest form, this may be stated as a warning: don't be fooled by the "democratic" nature of what is happening. As Geoffrey Gause warns, "America's proclivity to assume that all democratic movements share its overall policy goals should have been exploded by the results of the Iraqi elections of 2005 and 2010 and by Hamas's victory in Palestine in 2006, but the enthusiasm with which the American political class met the Arab upheavals of 2011 indicates that these naive assumptions die hard."[4]

At a deeper level, this lens makes European history a template for the Middle East and implies that the important questions are how to expedite matters so we can get the Arabs to Runnymede, Augsburg, and, ultimately, Philadelphia or Brussels, more quickly. Beyond the obvious geographical and historical projection inherent in such a view, there lies the greater conceit that Western civic and political values are the lodestar to which the aspirations of all men tend. As Sir Michael Howard, among many others, has observed, they are not.[5] The West is not universal. Whatever the future of freedom may be, to paraphrase Fareed Zakaria, Muslim notions of political freedom are distinct from 21st century American notions of it.[6] This is not to denigrate the idea that certain modalities of freedom (i.e., from tyranny) are universal aspirations of man. We are not projecting anything when we share in the elation of a people that throws off its tyrant. It is to assert that notions of freedom, especially civic or political freedom, are constructs of their time and place. They are informed by history, philosophy, culture, and perhaps most of all, cult, i.e., religion. Indeed it is the assertion of Carl Schmitt that

> all significant [Western] concepts of the modern theory of the state are secularized theological concepts not only because of their historical development—in which they were transferred from theology to the theory of the state, whereby, for example, the omnipotent god became the omnipotent lawgiver—but also because of their systematic structure, the recognition of which is necessary for a sociological consideration of these concepts.[7]

Why would it not be true that Islam's concepts of the state derive ultimately from Islamic theology?

Joseph Pieper, another German philosopher, captured the truth of this with his much more than

---

[4] F. Gregory Gause III, "Don't Just Do Something, Stand There!" *Foreign Policy*, December 21, 2011, http://www.foreignpolicy.com/articles/2011/12/21/america_arab_spring_do_nothing?page=full (accessed October 10, 2012).

[5] Michael Howard, "America and the World" (lecture, Annual Lewin Lecture at Washington University, St. Louis, MO, April 5, 1984).

[6] Fareed Zakaria, *The Future of Freedom* (New York, NY: Norton, 2003), 120-160. That the Islamic world's notions of freedom in the 21st century are substantially different from our own is the subject of chapter 4.

[7] Carl Schmitt, *Political Theology: Four Chapters on the Concept of Sovereignty*, trans. George Schwab (Chicago, IL: The University of Chicago Press, 1985), 36.

etymological observation that "cult is the basis of culture."[8] This is not obvious. One can spend a lifetime practicing common law and know nothing of its origins in the canon law of the Catholic Church. Likewise, few who swear allegiance to our constitution, the third article of whose first amendment forbids Congress from making "any law respecting an establishment of religion, or prohibiting the free exercise thereof" understand its structuralist Christian basis or discern its bias against a conception of political-religion such as Islam's.

The return of the Arab world to Islamic law will be one of the principal fruits of the Arab Spring. It is therefore worth taking a moment to de-universalize (i.e., particularize) the notion of freedom and to note how differently the concept is understood by Western and Islamic society. Man in Western society is legally free to do more or less as he likes morally so long as it does not impinge on others. Religious and not legal authority legislates, enforces, and penalizes in the sphere of morality. That it ought not to be the business of civil society to legislate morality has been a cornerstone of Western law since the enlightenment. This separation has never been viewed, perhaps, as ideal but it is in keeping both with the essentially apolitical nature of Christianity and with the exigencies of multi-confessional polities such as America's. Though most continue to view adultery, for example, as wrong, we see no role for the state in preventing it and little for punishing it besides, indirectly, awarding alimony at law to divorcees. In Islamic culture, informed by Sharia law that provides the basis for both personal and civic morality, such a definition of liberty is libertine and the notion of the separation of religion and state is foreign. While no one in Islam would dispute that man is capable of choosing wrong, that he ought not to do so is a given not just of moral but of civic life. I.e., it ought to be someone's job to stop him. While whose job exactly that ought to be is a subject of some variance within Islamic history and practice, it is universally agreed that no one in a Muslim society ought to have the liberty to do what is wrong, no matter how little

---

[8] Joseph Pieper, *Leisure as the Basis of Culture*, trans. Gerald Marsbury (South Bend, IN: St. Augustine's Press 1998), 65-76.

6

it may seem to hurt others.[9]   Human liberty exists within a moral framework and civil liberties are likewise bounded by explicit moral and religious law. This may mean that adulterers will be stoned more frequently in the days ahead and it will be challenging for us to watch. There will be those who see it as a step backward that we cannot stamp out such practices like the British were able to stamp out sati in India. Unlike the Raj, however, we are in no position to superimpose our law on local law in the Islamic world. Rather, we must view what is at stake in the current politics of the Middle East as those stakes and those politics are for the people of the Middle East *without regard to how they may be for us*. As Gause puts it, "if America is focused on remaking the domestic politics of transitioning Arab states in its own image, U.S. policy will inevitably fail."[10]

Removing ourselves from the picture is also the chief aim of removing the second unhelpful lens from our view of the Arab Spring. It is a corollary to the first and it is the tendency to view everything in the Muslim world as being part of a broader clash of our civilization with theirs. Such a phenomenon may well be occurring both at a grand Toynbeean level and more concretely in cities of Northern Europe and the schools of Southern France but it must not color our view of what is going on in the Middle East. The events of the Arab Spring are nothing if not internal matters that, if anything, amount to a clash within Islamic Civilization. Critically, we must not discern that resurgent traditional Islamic mores and practices are somehow a threat to Western Civilization. We may see them as a threat (or not) to Islamic Civilization but civilizations are not their brother's keeper. They will be distasteful and even run deeply counter to some of our most cherished principles. Nonetheless, our proper response will be to strengthen our own society and ensure that it remains otherwise. Once again, we cannot see these matters objectively if we can only see them as being about us. As Ken Pollack says, "The United States should

---

[9] Michael Cook, *Forbidding Wrong in Islam: An Introduction* (New York, NY: Cambridge University Press, 2003), 11-22.

[10] Gause, "Don't Just Do Something, Stand There!" *Foreign Policy.*

define the new regional struggle as one based on internal politics and the aspirations of the people of the region."[11]

The Arab Spring is an intra-civilizational affair and we must view it as such. That said, Huntington's theory of order within civilizations and specifically the importance of establishing a core state to arbitrate that order has considerable application to our analysis and will merit a closer examination below.[12] Before we consider the impact of the Arab Spring on Islam as a civilization, however, we must consider its impact on the countries in which it is occurring.

Before we consider what has happened in Tunis, Libya, and Egypt, or what is currently happening in Syria, we must begin with a consideration of what happened nine and a half years ago in Iraq. The narrative has been told countless ways. It has been seen as our greatest moment and our greatest folly. In context, it is neither. It simply is and we overly credit ourselves by a wide margin if we believe we knew what we were doing there in the realm of third order effects.

The United States toppled the Arab World's leading secular tyrant and proceeded to rebuild the country's political system in such a way as to be representative. When we did this, we transgressed the unwritten law of Sunni Arab Islam, in force since the days of Saladin, which says Sunnis ought to be empowered and Shia must be under Sunni rule. We enfranchised the majority for the first time in the history of the nation-state of Iraq and the Ottoman *velayats* that had preceded it for centuries. In so doing, we empowered Iran to expand its sphere of influence and pursue its bid to be the region's hegemon, a role it played briefly under the Abassids in the 10th century but for centuries prior to the coming of Islam in the

---

[11] Kenneth M. Pollack, "America's Second Chance and the Arab Spring," *Foreign Policy,* December 5, 2011, http://www.foreignpolicy.com/articles/2011/12/05/americas_second_chance?page=0,2 (accessed October 10, 2012).

[12] Samuel P. Huntington, *The Clash of Civilizations and the Remaking of World Order* (New York, NY: Simon and Schuster, 1996), 40-45. Huntington is not without his critics and this monograph purposefully eschews any discussion of a clash between Western and Islamic Civilization. Nonetheless, his discussion of the nature of civilizational identity in chapter 2 of this book and his assertion that the civilizational is the paradigm for international order is the authoritative narrative of the paradigm, whatever its merits.

7th century.[13] In fact, not since the Mongols under Helegu invaded Baghdad and installed a Shia ruler in their wake in the 13th century had Shia been empowered in Iraq, part of the Arab heartland.[14]

Sunnis across the Arab and non-Arab Muslim world came as jihadists to right the wrong and teach the Shia and the American Mongols a lesson. They came from the poorer Arab countries though not all were poor. They, and their cause, were financed largely by the wealthy countries of the Gulf. Not since the Afghan jihad against the Russians had the fires of jihad been so stoked. In a region with a demographic bulge of youth, little going on in the way of useful economic or social activity, it was not difficult to fuel.[15] Zawahiri and Zarqawi had a heated exchange of letters over the question of whom it was more important to kill indiscriminately, Americans or Shia. Zarqawi, the man in the arena, had the final word and focused on the Shia.[16] But the Shia fought back and Iran helped them. The United States, for a number of reasons, pursued a laissez-faire policy, hoping the two sides would exhaust themselves, but eventually intervened with the surge and the Anbar awakening. It was enough to kill the ringleaders on both sides but exhaustion also played an underestimated role.

The exhausted Jihadis went home to Syria and Libya, Tunis, Egypt, and Yemen and they are playing a seminal role in the ongoing birth of the Arab Spring.[17] This is not to say that Iraq veterans are the only seeds of the Arab Spring. They are not the ones who upset the apple cart of Bou Aziz in Sidi Bou Saeed or the ones who filled Tahrir Square with impassioned youth. But there is little doubt that in the initial years of Iraq, the U.S. wrought extraordinary concessions and even outright abouts-face on key policies from Arab leaders who feared they might be next and who had good reason to dread the return of those veterans to their home countries. Time will tell in what other ways Iraq has been in the chain of

---

[13] Nicholas Pelham, *A New Muslim Order: The Shia and the Middle East Sectarian Crisis* (New York: NY, I.B. Tauris, 2008), 26.

[14] Ibid., x.

[15] Jayshree Bajoria, "Demographics of Arab Protests: An Interview with Ragui Assaad, Professor, Humphrey School of Public Affairs, University of Minnesota" *Council on Foreign Relations*, February 14, 2011, http://www.cfr.org/egypt/demographics-arab-protests/p24096 (accessed May 12, 2012).

[16] Guido Steinberg, "Jihadi Salafism and the Shi'is: Remarks about the Intellectual Roots of anti-Shi'ism" in *Global Salafism*, ed. Meijer, 122-124.

[17] Ian Black, "The Libyan Islamic Fighting Group: From al-Qaida to the Arab Spring," *The Guardian*, 5 September 2011, http://www.guardian.co.uk/world/2011/sep/05/libyan-islamic-fighting-group-leaders (accessed September 5, 2011).

causality for the events of the Arab Spring but this point it seems self-serving and far from proven to imagine that the example of democracy and self-determination set in Iraq had a sort of domino effect that led to the Arab Spring. It is a long way from Baghdad to Tunis.

The Failure of Pan-Arabism

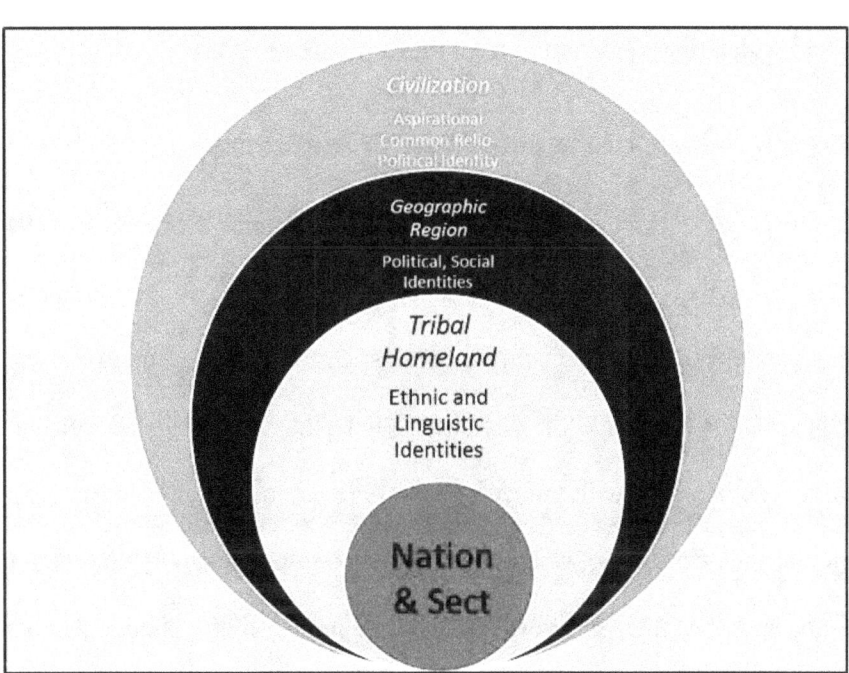

Pan-Arabism is a Syrian-born secular, meta-narrative of aspirational Arab transnational identity. Though undernoted throughout with Sunni Islam and its pre-modern notions of Islamic unity, it was thoroughly secular in nature and many of its leading lights were Christians and avowedly non-religious Muslims.[18] Though it began in the 19th century, it was in the First World War the Arabs had grown independence-minded enough to work with the British to overthrow Ottoman domination. They did not hate Turks as such nor did they resent having a Caliph. In fact, it is the lack of a Caliph in Islam that is considered socio-political chaos *(fitna)*, a state much to be avoided according to classical and modern

---

[18] Vali Nasr, *The Shia Revival: How Conflicts in Islam Will Shape the Future* (New York, NY: Norton, 2006), 90-93.

10

Islamic teaching.[19] Rather, Turkish rule had become lazy, indifferent, bigoted, and ineffective. As T.E.

Lawrence put it, "Turkish rule was gendarme rule, and Turkish political theory as crude as its practice.

The Turks taught the Arabs that the interests of a sect were higher than those of patriotism: that the petty

concerns of the province were more than nationality."[20] Additionally, the increasing penetration of

Western missionaries, archeologists, and speculators, had opened Arab eyes to a world beyond the

Ottomans, a world to which they could strive were they only free to do so.[21]

Nasserism and the Failure of the United Arab Republic

Following his perceived victory against the European Colonial powers in the 1956 Suez War in

which Harry Truman effectively aborted the combined British and French Suez campaign mid-stride,

Egyptian president Gamal Abd an-Nasser achieved almost godlike status in the Arab world.[22] Syria,

under President Shukri al-Quwatli and Prime Minister Khaled al-Azem made overtures to Nasser to enter

into a national union. Yemen eventually joined as a confederate to the union as well. For three years,

from Feb. 1, 1958, until Sept. 28, 1961, when Syria pulled out after a coup by disgruntled Baathist

officers, the cultural capitals of the Arab world were united politically.[23] Though formed in royalist

opposition to the republican Egyptian-Syrian union, from February 14, 1958 to August 2, 1958, the

cousin Hashemite monarchs of Iraq and Jordan also formed a union.[24] Though neither union, in the end,

lasted or amounted to a great deal in the long term, this period represented the high water mark and the

highest level of achievement of the aspirations of secular pan-Arabism.

Having failed to keep Syria or Yemen in a transnational union, Nasser in 1967 engineered a

second war against Israel which again appealed to pan-Arab unity by including Syria, Iraq, Jordan, and

---

[19] Bernard Lewis, *Islam in History: Ideas, Men, and Events in the Middle East* (New York, NY: Library Press, 1973), 258-263.

[20] T.E. Lawrence, *Seven Pillars of Wisdom: A Triumph*, (New York, NY: Anchor Books, 1991), 44.

[21] Michael B. Oren, *Power, Faith, and Fantasy: America in the Middle East 1776 to the Present* (New York, NY: Norton, 2007), 257-324.

[22] Kenneth Pollack, *Arabs at War* (Omaha, NE: University of Nebraska Press, 2002), 44-45.

[23] Malcolm H. Kerr, *The Arab Cold War* (New York, NY: Oxford University Press, 1971), 44-95.

[24] Kerr, *The Arab Cold War*.

11

other states. Unlike his success in 1956 against the British and French, this war was a *nekba,* a catastrophe. He offered to resign after the complete Arab defeat just days after the war began.[25]

Though his resignation was turned down by the overwhelming sentiment of the Egyptian people, Nasser never recovered his superhuman status in the Arab world. At the same time, a quietly growing trend of Islamic fundamentalists with close ties to the Wahabbis of Saudi Arabia who called themselves the Muslim Brothers split from his regime and began spreading a new narrative first in Egypt and soon throughout the Arab world of Islamism, a movement with many of the same goals as pan-Arabism but with an explicitly Islamist worldview.[26]

The Rise of Islamist Transnational Identity

After the October War of 1973, it was clear that the secular and nationalist order had not delivered on its promises to the elites of the Muslim world, Sunni and Shia. Their societies remained backwards and the indignities of a series of defeats by tiny Israel and heavy-handed policies by the West were never far from mind. The grand prospects that nationalism and socialism had engendered in the minds of the elites had never been shared by the common people, however. All they saw was the same corrupt elite as before, only now it didn't even maintain the façade of being pious. Islam has, after all, a political component as well as a religious one; neither makes sense without the other. Indeed, Karen Armstrong has called politics the single "sacrament" of Islam.[27] The notion of a transnational Muslim unity that orders the world by faith rather than nationality goes back to the heart of Islam's formation in antiquity and in modernity to Jamal al-Din Afghani in the late 19th century.[28] Both *the cuius regio* of religion according to the national sovereign implicit in a Westphalian order and that very division into nation states run counter to deeply rooted aspirations of Islam.

---

[25] Pollack, *Arabs at War,* 86-87.

[26] Richard P. Mitchell, *The Society of the Muslim Brothers,* (New York, NY: Oxford University Press, 1969), 105-162.

[27] Karen Armstrong, *Islam: A Short History* (New York: Modern Library, 2002), xii.

[28] Center for Islam and Science, "Voices", Afghani, http://www.cis-ca.org/voices/a/afghni.htm (accessed August 15, 2012).

In Iran, these attitudes expressed themselves in deep resentment against the Westernized and secular Shah. Ayatollah Khomeini was able to tap into this resentment and offer the promise of something better. His overthrow of the Shah 1979 was doubly revolutionary because it was both Islamist and Shia. Nonetheless, Khomeini envisioned an Islamism that was not sectarian. His movement was not Shia Islamist but was explicitly pan-Islamist and inclusive of both Sunni and Shia Islamist aspirations. These aspirations included working for social justice, including the overthrow of secular rulers, defeating Israel, and dealing a blow to the West that could cause it to reassess its stances in the Middle East.[29] These aspirations were shared by Shia and Sunni Islamist alike and work toward them across sectarian lines was not just possible but normal.

The line between Shia and Sunni did not, by this burgeoning set of pan-Islamist aspirations, disappear. Outside of Iran, people of the Middle East retained an ability both to sympathize with the Iranian Revolution and its stance against the West and Israel and to hold it suspect. No one held it more suspect than Iran's neighbors, especially Saddam Hussein.

The Failure of Saddam in the Gulf War

The rise of pan-Islamism as a counter-narrative to pan-Arabism was especially tumultuous in Iraq under Saddam Hussein. A Sunni ruler over a country that had a Shia majority and deep ties to Iran, Saddam had a great deal to fear from revolutionary Iran. His Kurdish populations in the North spoke a language close to Persian, had deep ties across the border, and harbored a deep desire for independence. Meanwhile, his Shia Arab population looked to Iran's overthrow of the Shah as an example they might be able to follow by overthrowing Saddam. Iran actively encouraged and aided both movements. Saddam was not entirely without justification in declaring war against Iran and his effort was widely supported by the people and leadership of the Arab world.

---

[29] Bernard Haykel, "On the Nature of Salafi thought and Action: Appendix al-Qaeda's Creed and Path" in *Global Salafism: Islam's New Religious Movement*, ed. Roel Meijer (New York, NY: Columbia University Press, 2009), 33-51.

When the war ended in what was effectively a draw, Saddam deeply believed that the Arab world owed him something for his costly war. He had ample rhetoric from sympathetic Arab countries to believe himself their champion as the new Nasser and the pan-Arab leader in the lead of resistance against both Islamism and Shiism. When he invaded Kuwait on the not entirely fabricated pretense of it stealing his oil, however, he exposed a divide between the rulers of the Arab world and the people. The rulers, with only a few exceptions, aligned with the West against him. The people were for him, and for Islamic reasons. Peter Demant argues that his very defiance of the U.N., viewed as the Western world order, won him approval of Islamic authorities despite his secularism. Some of them even called for his crowning as their caliph.[30] When he was defeated by the West in coalition with most Arab regimes, popular and religious hatred of those regimes increased over the next twelve years.

The Overthrow of Saddam in Desert Storm

When, in 2003, the U.S. returned to Iraq to finish off Saddam's regime, it had the support of neither the people nor the regimes of the Arab world. Though Sunni Arab governments knew he was an SoB, he was their SoB. Iran, deeply inimical to us, was the only Middle Eastern nation that delighted in his overthrow and it moved quickly to shore up its ties with Iraqi Shias. Though happy to have Iranian support in the sectarian violence that followed, Iraqi Shias had for the most part been unimpressed with Khomeinism and Iraqi Shiism, personified best by Ayatollah Sistani, had no taste for an Iranian style theocracy of *velayat-i-fiqh*. Sunnis, in Iraq and elsewhere, saw the fall of Saddam and the rise of Shia power in the Arab world as *fitna*, a chaos in the right order of the Muslim world. Salafists, Sunni Islamists who embrace violent jihad, from across the Arab world came to Iraq to restore Sunni and Arab dominance.

The post-Saddam chaos in Iraq revealed deep cracks in the façade of pan-Islamist unity. Usama Bin Laden's deputy, Ayman al-Zawahiri, sent a widely read letter to Abu Musab al-Zarqawi, the leader of

---

[30] Peter Demant, *Islam vs. Islamism: The Dilemma of the Muslim World*, (Westport, CT: Praeger, 2006), 132-133.

14

the jihadi Islamist resistance in Iraq. In this letter, he is highly critical of Zarqawis strategy of killing Shia qua Shia. Zawahiri argues that it is far more important to kill Americans and limit the killing of Shia to those with the temerity to seek power.[31] Such a subtle distinction showed the degree to which unity of any kind was strongly lacking.

The Fate of Asad

Syria has long declared itself to be guardian of Arab unity and its claim to be "the beating heart of pan-Arabism" was well-accepted in the Arab world.[32] Now, Asad is widely seen as a Shiite with the temerity to seek to hold on to power. Syrian public intellectual and Sunni Nabil Fayyad has long stressed that it is precisely Syria's diversity, including robust and empowered Christian, Alawi, Druze and Ismaili

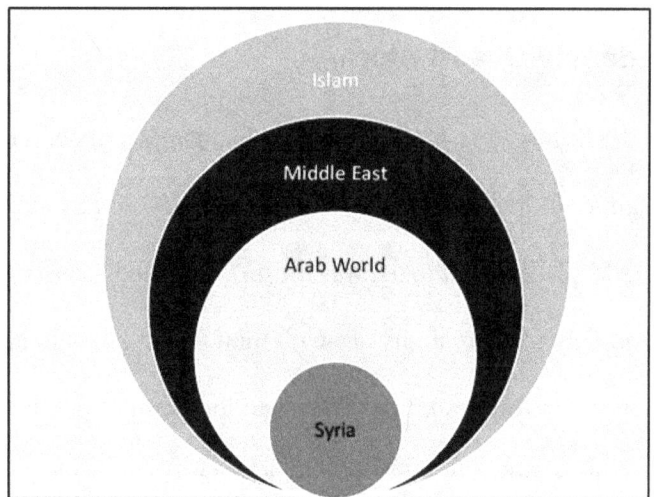

religious populations that created the polished and cosmopolitan capital of an Arab world that was pluralistic and inclusive. Fayyad sees this multiplicity of perspectives on Arab-ness as being central to Syria and its claim to moderate the Arab world. He distinguished Syria from Egypt in this regard. Though Cairo is the other great capital of the Arab world, Egypt's 90% Sunni population is balanced only by a weak and un-empowered Coptic Christian minority. There are no other elements to color Egyptian

---

[31] Guido Steinberg, "Jihadi Salafism and the Shi'is: Remarks about the Intellectual Roots of anti-Shi'ism" in *Global Salafism*, ed. Meijer, 122-124.

[32] Adeed Dawisha, "Requiem for Arab Nationalism," *Middle East Quarterly* 10, no. 1 (Winter 2003): 25-41.

society. Thus Egypt, though the Arabs' leading light under Nasser, ultimately succumbed to the narrowness of Sunni Islam's intellectual climate, according to Fayyad. His view is shared widely among liberals and minorities in Syria that Syria's minoritarian Alawi government and general privileging of minorities are essential to maintaining a cosmopolitan and diverse center of the Arab world.[33] Islamists also understand that diverse minority views are essential to propping up a notion of Arab unity that is not religious-based, i.e., pan-Arabism. But they want to see it replaced with an explicitly Islamist notion of identity and unity.

The Failure of Pan-Islamism

The emergence in all the countries of the Arab Spring of powerful Islamist parties is perhaps the most important political trend in the Muslim world. In the West, it is common to see the emergence of Islamism as pitting forces of liberal modernity against forces of reactionary traditionalism. It is certainly this to the highly limited extent that there are liberal forces of any strength in Islamic societies but a focus on this polarization misses the main import of Islamism to the Muslim world. Islamism became a mainstream alternative with the failure of Nasser. Since the Iranian Revolution, it has become the dominant meta-narrative of the region. When Syria falls, it will become the exclusive grand unifying principle of the Middle East. Until the past decade, this narrative was unifying and non-sectarian. Now, with the division of the Middle East and beyond into ever less tolerant Sunni and Shia camps, non-sectarian Islamism, or pan-Islamism is nearing a point of failure as a narrative. In its stead has emerged, on the Sunni side, an Islamism that is exclusively Sunni.

Though we have become accustomed in the past decade to thinking of Shia and Sunni in opposition, and not without historic justification, it is important to remember that The Iranian revolution was never intended to be just for Shias. From the beginning, Revolutionary Iran exported its doctrine of

---

[33] Nabil Fayyad is a Syrian Public Intellectual and Social Critic. The author lived with Mr. Fayyad while on a Fulbright Fellowship in Damascus from 2005-2006 and these views are from unpublished personal notes of conversations held during that time.

revolution abroad in a non-sectarian manner. Israel and the West had long existed as the enemy to both pan-Arabism and Islamism without regard to differences between Sunni, Shia, Arab, or Persian. When Iran moved into the scene, it created pan-Islamism that was a joining of Shia and Sunni Islamism against Israel and the West. From humble origins in Musa al-Sadr's internal development-focused Amal, the Iranian Revolutionary Guards Corps created Hezbollah not just as a defense force for Shia in Lebanon during that country's civil war in the early 80s but as a force aligned with Sunni Islamist movements against Israel and the West.

Although a Sunni organization, Hamas's principal backer was Iran, the Islamist alternative to the Arab Nationalist Palestine liberation Organization (PLO) and its largest faction, Fatah.[34] Based, until recently, in Syria when the sectarian overtones to that conflict caused it to move elsewhere, Hamas represents the first rank of Sunni militancy against Israel. That this first rank of Sunni militancy should receive its principal funding from Iran says a great deal about the salience within the Arab world of the powerful notion of pan-Islamism. It also says a great deal about the vacuum of leadership in the Sunni world.

The Rise of Turkey and the AKP

Though Iran was the leading Islamist force prior to the Spring of 2011, the vacuum of Islamist leadership it filled was never perfect. The Sunni Muslim Brotherhood had long held a prestigious place and since the 1920s has grown in numbers and strength. But without the authority of national power, it had been a force *in potentiam* with little ability to lead. Likewise, the panoply of extremist Islamist groups, nearly all explicitly anti-Shia, have risen in prominence but not permanence throughout the Middle East and South Asia. Because of their shared enemies in pro-Western Arab governments and the

---

[34] Fares Akram and Isabel Kershner, "Hamas Premier Visits Iran in Sign of Strong Relations," *The New York Times*, 10 February 2012, http://www.nytimes.com/2012/02/11/world/middleeast/hamas-premier-ismail-haniya-visits-iran.html (accessed August 15, 2012).

money and legitimacy of state sponsorship it brought to the table, Iran was able to maintain, if not leadership, considerable influence even with groups diametrically opposed to Shiism such as al-Qaeda. A real contender has begun to emerge in the years since 2005 in the newly non-secular Turkey under President Erdogan's AKP. This dynamic emergence of Turkey has had two facets. As a model for emerging Islamist movements in the Middle East, the AKP in particular and the "Turkish model" generally stands as "a form of Islamism that is compatible with the democratic process that is able to deliver and that is granted due recognition and legitimacy both in Turkey and internationally", according to Hassan Mneimneh. The Hudson Institute scholar presciently pointed out in 2011—and has since been fully justified by events—that it was the tactical success of the party to succeed in the face of democratic processes that Arab Islamists wished to emulate rather than its subtlety or restraint from overt religiosity.[35]

Nonetheless, the rise of Turkey over the past decade to regional power status has significantly leveled the playing field for Iran. Turkey has responded to its new economic power by seeking a new role for itself in the Islamic *Umma*. Distancing itself from the US and Europe while simultaneously deepening ties with the Muslim world, Turkey has confronted Israel on several public occasions and emerged on the scene of Islamic development and finance. No one appreciates the significance of the new strongman so much as the Iranians who, speaking through a mouthpiece in Iraq, describe the revival of Ottoman Imperialism as "the most dangerous trend in the Islamic World."[36] It is interesting that they should do so. Turkey has cultivated neighborly ties with Iran, and, while it was still politically possible to do so, with Iran's ally Syria and has kept itself relatively aloof from the international churn against Iran's nuclear program. Nonetheless, Iran sees the writing on the wall in Turkey's inevitable alignment with the Sunni powers, especially the emerging coalition of GCC nations, and it reads the writing of history,

---

[35]Hassan Mneimneh, "The "Turkish Model" in Arab Islamism: Rejection or Emulation?" The Hudson Institute's Center on Islam, Democracy, and the Future of the Muslim World, April 22, 2011, http://www.currenttrends.org/research/detail/the-turkish-model-in-arab-islamism-rejection-or-emulation (accessed September 1, 2012).

[36] This quote, attributed to President Maliki, was shared with SAMS students by a senior military guest speaker who may not be named in respect of rules of non-attribution.

remembering the long period of Imperial rivalry—and sectarian enmity—between Sunni Ottomans and the Shia Safavids from the 16th through the 18th centuries.

The revival of a powerful neighbor in the land of the former Ottoman Empire has concerned descendants of the Safavid Empire in Iran, which is to say that Turkey's return to the fold of explicitly Islamic countries has revived something of the competition between the two great nations. This competition is first one of nationalism and history and only distantly one of religion. This is not the case the rise of Salafism, another Islamist phenomenon that began to appear in the mid-90s, this one with ideological and financial links to Iran's regional rival Saudi Arabia and with no tolerance for diversity of sectarian affiliation.

The Rise of Political Salafism

In its October 2012 report on the Fundamentalist component of Syria's Opposition, the International Crisis Group identified Salafis as "part of the profound identity crisis [The Syrian Conflict] has produced."[37] They are just as much part of the identity crisis of the broader Arab Spring and of greater Islamic Civilization in which the Syrian conflict is so centrally nested. Salafis are those who follow the traditions of the *salaf,* the early Sunni Muslims of the 7th Century. They make concerted efforts to act and think as they understand early Sunnis did and they are in the habit of correcting those Muslims who do not.[38] Shiism has a great variety of subtle differences from Sunni Islam and the Salafist does not fail to notice them. Salafis are exclusivists. Those who do not share their regard for the right ways are in grave error. Those who believe that error is so great as to demerit its holder the title of Muslim are called *Takfiris,* those who declare others unbelievers. Given the penalties prescribed by Islamic Law and traditional practice for unbelief, Salafis and *Takfiris* constitute a difficult bloc to

---

[37] International Crisis Group, "Tentative Jihad: Syria's Fundamentalist Opposition", Executive Summary, *Middle East Report N°131,* http://www.crisisgroup.org/en/regions/middle-east-north-africa/egypt-syria-lebanon/syria/131-tentative-jihad-syrias-fundamentalist-opposition.aspx (accessed October 15, 2012).
[38] Ibid.

accommodate in any broader Islamist coalition.[39] Further making matters difficult, one of the key tenets of Salafists is that political involvement, especially in democratic processes, is not in accordance with the acts of the early Muslims and, therefore, not properly Islamic. For the reasons given above, along with the fact that the Salafi movement is largely funded by the very similar Wahabbi strain of Islam that is dominant in oil-rich Saudi Arabia, Iran has never been able to count on pan-Islamist ententes with the Salafists. Even when it has succeeded in putting aside differences in order to work for a shared purpose (i.e., against a common enemy), each side has questioned whether it is working against or with the greater enemy. While the Muslim Brothers would be counted as fundamentalists in any other religion, within the spectrum of Islamic revival, they are usually described as moderates. And next to the Salafists, on a surprisingly wide spectrum of issues, they are.

Even if we don't count all the parts of the Islamic world where their jihadist incarnation is currently waging an insurgency, the Salafists are a major force in mainstream politics. En Egypt, though they initially loomed large in 2012's election with the surprise showing of their own candidate, their most important role there has turned out to be a voice of conservative conscience.[40] They are able to sway the Muslim Brotherhood away from more moderate positions. As we watch events unfold after Tahrir Square, observers will closely watch the extent to which Salafis are able move the center of gravity of the Muslim Brothers, and Egypt with them, ever further to the right.

Post-Saddam Sectarian War in Iraq

Though the rebirth of Islam in Turkey's identity poses questions as to the rightful leader of pan-Islamism and the development of Salafism proposse a narrowing of the definition of Islamism, it took an actual historical event to bring the whole narrative crashing down. That crisis was Saddam's overthrow in 2003 or rather, its aftermath. As we have seen. That Saddam fell in the first place was a blow to those

---

[39] Ibid.

[40] Hassan Mneimneh, "The Spring of a New Political Salafism?," *Current Trends in Islamist Ideology*, vol.12 (October 2011), http://www.currenttrends.org/research/detail/the-spring-of-a-new-political-salafism (accessed July 12, 2012).

20

who had come to conflate his political resistance to the West with their longing for a caliph to lead Islam religiously. That Shia were empowered following his departure was something else altogether. NPR commentator Deborah Amos has written an entire book documenting sentiments of Sunni eclipse in the post-2003 Arab World. Present among many of these sentiments is the notion that any gain for the Shia or the Kurds was by definition a loss for the Sunnis.[41] With this wide feeling of being marginalized in the civilization they felt it their divine right to rule, a narrative developed of blame and hatred not just for America and the West, the usual suspects, but for Iran and Shias in general. A feature of Islamism is that it places a person's faith prior in importance to his nationality. In the post-Saddam world, the definition of faith ceased to be Muslim and became, rather, Sunni or Shia. This occurred not only in the attitudes and actions of the *takfiri* jihadis terrorizing the Shia. It became the unofficial consensus of the Sunni Arab elite and street that something in the ominous shape of Vali Nasr's putative Shia revival is at hand.[42]

The 33 Day War

Hezbollah, rather than wait for events, has made itself master of them on a number of high profile occasions. None has been higher than its 33-day war with Israel in 2006. Though the war was dubious in its tactical outcome, analysts quickly came to see it as a strategic victory for Hezbollah. The Arab street came to see it as a victory for Arabs and Islam. The war may well come to be seen as the last pan-Islamic event in history. Though Hezbollah did all the fighting against the Israelis, the Arab elite and street was on its side. The Israelis compounded this by bombing Lebanon far north of Hezbollah-dominated areas and drawing the understandable ire of Sunnis and even Christians. To the extent that there were Christians and Druze who were ready to join Hezbollah, it could even be considered a last pan-Arab event.

---

[41] For one of many examples, see Deborah Amos, *Eclipse of the Sunnis: Power, Exile, and Upheaval in the Middle East* (New York, NY: PublicAffairs, 2010), 115.

[42] Nasr, *Shia Revival*.

Though there is nothing quite like a war to bring people together, the repercussions of this war only added to fears of a Shia revival. Such was the effusive outpouring of sentiment in the Arab street for Hezbollah's leadership that many incidences were reported of "conversions" to Shiism.[43] Although Sunni and Shia are but different approaches to the same religion, and conversion to and fro not proscribed by either, it is a relatively rare phenomenon. While it hardly became common following the war, the few notable examples of it merged in the Sunni narrative with discoveries of Shia proselytization and sent a wave of fear through the Arab elite.[44] Jordan's King Hussein expressed this fear when he warned of "a Shia Crescent stretching from Iran to the Mediterranean."[45] That Shia crescent will lose a vital connecting piece in Syria.

Long-Term Outcomes

Civilizational Division

If current trends continue unabated, the sub-civilizational divide between Sunni and Shia could become deeper. We understand Christianity as split into Latin American, Western, and Orthodox civilizations while we see Islam as one. Whatever differences are between the partisans (Shia) of Ali and orthodox (Sunni) Islam have not seemed to rise to the level of the civilizational. In view of the crisis within Islam that is becoming evident in the "Arab Spring", it may be time to reconsider this monolithic view of Islamic Civilization.

Much is lost in projecting terms from Western history like "Counter-reformation" or "Great Schism" onto Islam. The fact that they are capitalized makes them proper nouns – proper to a particular civilization and time. Furthermore, the very nature of Islam involves an inherent political element that

---

[43] Khalid Sindawi, "The Shiite Turn in Syria," *Current Trends in Islamist Ideology*, vol. 8 (June 2009), http://www.currenttrends.org/research/detail/the-shiite-turn-in-syria (accessed July 12, 2012).

[44] Khalid Sindawi, "Jordan's Encounter with Shi'ism," *Current Trends in Islamist Ideology*, vol. 10 (August 2010), http://www.currenttrends.org/research/detail/jordans-encounter-with-shiism (accessed July 9, 2012).

[45] Ian Black, "Fear of a Shia Full Moon," *The Guardian*, 26 January 2007, http://www.guardian.co.uk/world/2007/jan/26/worlddispatch.ianblack (accessed July 10, 2012).

22

makes any comparison with religious phenomena in Christianity grossly inadequate. Nonetheless, in our metaphorical lexicon, one of them is the closest approximation to what is going on in Islam today. The question is which one? The counter-reformation was an intra-civilizational reaction by Catholicism against the rise of Protestantism. The Great Schism saw the formation of two civilizations where there had previously been one.

Civilizations are not coterminous with religions but the degree of coterminity varies with the religion in question. Christianity, in Huntington's schematic, is the underlying religion of Western and Orthodox Civilization though few thought much about the commonality during the tense years of the Cold War. Pope and Patriarch may have excommunicated each other in the Great Schism of the 10th century that divided Western from Eastern (Orthodox) Christianity but the divide between the Hellenic East and the Roman West predated the Great Schism by at least 700 years, during almost all of which both halves of the Empire were Christian. Likewise, the West and Latin America, even if one considers the former as having a dominant Protestant ethos, share Western Christianity as their religion. Neither is religion by any means the crucial factor in comparing the civilization of the West with either those of Sub-Sahel Africa or Korea which are soon to be majority Protestant Christian. Religion is just one of many factors that form a region's civilization. History, ethnicity, sociology, and ideology all have equal weight with religion in forming the cultural, social, and political identity and outlook of a nation or bloc of nations and it is this *gestalt* identity which is civilizational.[46]

Civilizational identity for Muslims is considerably less a confluence of factors than for Christianity. This is due to the dual political and religious nature of Islam, and its world-wide quest for unity since the revival of Islamist ideology in the twentieth century. The fact that there are millions of Muslims living normal lives in Orthodox, Sinic, Latin American and Western Civilization is deeply troubling to an Islamist. He understands Islam as being a religion and a polity, a way of private, civic, and public life. In short, it is a civilization unto itself.

---

[46] Huntington, *Clash of Civilizations*, 40-45.

Yet "Islamic Civilization" is Arab-centric. Non-Arab Muslims may memorize the Koran in its entirety but as they do not speak Arabic, they do not understand what they have memorized outside of a few verses that are common cultural coin. British MP and writer Rory Stewart shared an incident of his walk across Afghanistan in which a young *hafiz,* a boy who had memorized the Koran, pronounced Rory's dog to be unclean, according to the Koran. When Rory asked him where it said that in the Koran, the boy sheepishly admitted he had no idea as he did not understand Arabic.[47]

This is not to say that today's Turks, Pakistanis, Central Asians, and Indonesians do not identify with Islamic Civilization which is, ultimately, egalitarian and inclusive. Each of these countries, and many others, feel that their people share in the patrimony of Islam as a universal religion that does not discriminate on the basis of color, ethnicity, or station in life. The failures of secular nationalist ideologies and attempts at identity formation pushed but this universal appeal is what pulled Arabs back from Nasser and Turks back from Ataturk.

Though one might expect such a thing to be said of in Iran, it is not precisely so. This is because Iran never defined Islamic civilization in the distinctly Arabic way that other regions to which Islam came did. Greater Persia, which included Iraq, is, after the Peninsular Arabs themselves, the eldest daughter of Islam. It was the first nation to fully embrace Islam after the Arab conquests. Egypt and North Africa did not become majority Muslim until the late middle ages and Greater Syria did not become majority Muslim until well into the modern era though, due to the proximity of Aramaic to Arabic, the linguistic transition was almost immediate in the Levant.

In Iran, language has always been a sticking point for Islamicization. While Persians converted to Islam accepted the Koran as sacred and immutable, and thus untranslatable, this fact did not grant superiority to the Arab culture. Even more important, though than language, for Greater Persia, is the messianic alternative version of Islam that emerged from members of Muhammad's family. Though Shia

[47] Rory Stewart, *The Places In Between* (London, UK: Picador, 2004), 127.

origins are largely obscured by the lack of documentation, we do know that it was in Iraq, in greater

Persia, that the partisans of Ali first established themselves institutionally. Lewis writes that

> new converts . . . brought with them, from their Judeo-Christian and Iranian backgrounds many religious
> ideas alien to primitive Islam. These new converts became Muslims; they did not become Arabs, still less
> aristocrats, and the expectations aroused in them by their new faith made them deeply resentful of the
> inferior social and economic status accorded to them by the dominant Arab aristocracy. These feelings
> were shared by both pious and discontented Arabs, especially those who suffered from the sharper
> economic and social differentiation that came with conquest and riches. Many of the new converts were
> familiar with both political and religious legitimism. They were readily attracted by the claims of the house
> of the Prophet [proto-Shia sectarians], which seemed to offer an end to the injustices of the existing order
> and a fulfillment of the promise of Islam.[48]

He also notes that the transition from the initial Umayyad dynasty of Syria to the subsequent Abbasid

dynasty in Iraq was accompanied by a shift to greater roles for non-Arab elites, especially bureaucrats of

Persian society.[49] Although the initial promise of the Abassids for a perfect Islamic society was soon

dispelled, and Iran was a thoroughly Sunni country until the Safavid dynasty emerged in 1501, Iran

remained distinct from the rest of the Sunni world.

With the Safavids, whose founder, Ismail, adopted the title *Padishah-i-Iran*, "Persian Emperor",

the Persian language and Shia religion united in forming a distinct civilization throughout Central Asia,

reaching up into the Caucasus and across into Afghanistan and Baluchistan. Though the Ottomans took

on the mantle of the Sunni world's core state and took Iraq from the Safavids in the 18th century bringing

the principal Shia cities of Najaf and Karbala under their Sunni suzerainty, the Shia faith had strong roots

in Iraq and strong ties to the coreligionists in Iran.

Since the resurgence of Shia political power and Iranian influence in Iraq and Lebanon, and, to a

lesser extent, Syria, the threat of a Shia Crescent has frightened Sunnis precisely because Iran in particular

and Shias in general have never been full members in the consensus definition of Islamic Civilization. As

the Sunni Arab world reasserts its Islamic identity in the Arab Spring and Syria becomes once again a

Sunni power cutting off Lebanon from Iraq and Iran, two civilizational possibilities emerge. Shia Islam

can remain a sub-civilizational division within Islamic Civilization or it can emerge fully clad in its own

---

[48] Lewis, *Islam in History*, 240.
[49] Ibid., 247-248.

civilizational raiment. In either case, Iran will be the core of either the subdivision or of the civilization. It is true that Iran would like to be the core state of all of Islamic Civilization and that in the past decade, this has looked more likely than at any time since the early days of the Abbasid caliphate in the 9th century. But such ambitions are now finished. The Sunni Spring and its emergence of Sunni Islamist regimes, along with the sharp decline in Iran's "soft power" have seen to that.

It is difficult to see, given the above, how Shia Islam could rise to levels of unity and cohesion that could lead again to a bi-polar Islamic world. There will be no Shia anti-caliphate like the Fatmids of 13th century Egypt. There will be two separate and culturally distinct Shia zones. Each will be strong but each will be balanced on several sides by Sunni powers that will ultimately prevent the sort of unity and identity formation that could lead to an alternative core grouping for Islam.

Westphalian Peace

If Sunni and Shia are bound, then, to civilizationally hang together, why might they not move toward a Western ordering? An oft-quoted phrase of Middle Eastern studies' doyenne Bernard Lewis is that the Middle East, having caught a Christian disease, i.e., war of religion, might seek a Christian remedy.[50] It is important to classify this disease and cure as Western rather than Christian, however. The divide between Orthodox and Western Christianity, itself based on pre-existing civilizational and geographical separation did indeed lead to the formation of distinct Christian civilizations. What Lewis is referring to is the divide inside the West between Protestant and Catholic. He believes it eminently possible that an indigenous *cuius regio* order could emerge in the Middle East.[51] His argument has the force of history. The early modern period, i.e., from the establishment of the Safavid dynasty at the dawn of the 16th century and the founding of Iran as a Shia state until the collapse of the Ottoman Empire, witnessed precisely such a phenomenon. The Persian and Ottoman Empires ruled the greater Middle East between them. The Arab world came almost entirely under the latter's Sunni domain while Persia

---

[50] Lewis, *Islam in History*, 406-420.
[51] Lewis, *Islam in History*.

exercised important influence east into Central Asia, Afghanistan and India. Yet the parallel is not precise. In the first place, both were Empires rather than states and both included vast numbers of the other's sect. In fact, the Safavid Empire was always a minoritarian Shia realm. Turkey, the heartland of the erstwhile Ottoman Empire includes 15-20 million Shia Alevis and Alawis, roughly a quarter of its population.[52] Unlike in Christendom during its divisions between Protestant and Catholic, the Safavids made Iran itself a Shia domain but did not extend Shiism throughout their realm any more than the Ottomans sought with any energy to convert its Shia areas to Sunnism.

However imprecise, the Middle East could emerge from a sectarian bloodbath that pitted Sunni against Shia with an order in which each state was, after likely exchanges of population, either Sunni or Shia according to either the sovereign clan of that state or the majority population. Indeed, the flight of Shia from Iraq a few years ago and of Sunnis from Syria now may presage such a division. Certainly there is something implicit in representative democracy that makes a state with a Shia majority seek to have a Shia government and foreign policy.

Many believe that such an order can never emerge, however. Former Iraqi official and moderate pan-Islamist Ayyad Alawi sees such a Westphalian order of Muslim democracy as

> a pathway to a secular and ultimately Western definition of the political rather than a re-expression of the political in Islam…democracy is unlikely to resolve the conundrum which Muslims face when they were dealing with the political: the need to evolve a privileged place for the sacred in the structuring of the Islamic political order.[53]

Neo-Ottoman Restoration of Islamic Civilization

No country is better poised, in the long run, to restructure Islamic political order than Turkey. President Erdogan and his AKP party are the embodiment of a new elite in Turkey, one that draws its

---

[52] Jeffrey Gettleman, "As Syria War Roils, Unrest Among Sects Hits Turkey," *The New York Times*, 4 August 2012, http://www.nytimes.com/2012/08/05/world/middleeast/turkish-alawites-fear-spillover-of-violence-from-syria.html?pagewanted=1&src=recg (accessed August 15, 2012).

[53] Ayyad Alawi, *The Crisis of Islamic Civilization*. (Hartford, CT: Yale University Press, 2009), 185.

support from the deeply Islamic Anatolian heartland rather than the western and Westernized coast.[54] The strength of Erdogan has been his ability to take that deeply traditional and Islamic Anatolian population and remold it as "pro-free-enterprise, pro-Western, and pro-Globalization" according to Asaf Savas Akat.[55] This promise of an ability to create a new face for Sunni Islamism that grapples with the modern world productively may be the greatest hope for Islamic Civilization.

It gives Turkey the chance to lead Sunni Islam – and to lead it away from Salafism. This portends the possibility of considerable power for Turkey in the not too distant term. Huntington observed that Islamic civilization lacked a core state, a concept he defines as a state whose "power attracts those who are culturally similar and repels those who are culturally different."[56] In his schematic of emerging world order, core states would be the foci of spheres of influence in the post-bipolar world after the collapse of the Soviet Union. To Huntington, a civilization is an extended family and, like older members of a family, core states provide their relatives with both support and discipline."[57] He observed that Turkey has the "history, population, middle level of economic development, national coherence, and military tradition and competence to be the core state of Islam" if only it could move away from its secular legacy of Ataturk.[58] In the intervening 17 years since 1995's publication of Huntington's thesis, Turkey has done nothing if not define itself as more Islamic and less secular. The Justice and Freedom Party, the AKP, may well have accepted the truth of Huntington's civilizational reasons for pessimism about Turkey's accession into the European Union but turned this civilizational fact into an asset.[59]

Fantastic as it sounded when the world read of the caliphate in the wild-eyed fancies of a Bin Laden, Turkey could gain a good deal by re-establishing the Caliphate in modern form as an EU of Muslim States under its benign domination. Such a union could be highly stabilizing to the region. The

---

[54] David P. Goldman, *How Civilizations Die: (And Why Islam Is Dying Too)* (Washington, DC: Regnery, 2011), 68.

[55] Akat, Asaf Savas. Interview with David P. Goldman. Ibid., 66.

[56] Huntington, *Clash of Civilizations*, 156.

[57] Ibid., 156.

[58] Huntington, *Clash of Civilizations*, 178.

[59] Ibid., 162.

Arab League will become even less important than it previously has been (with the notable exception of its uniting against Syria in 2011) and neither the OIC nor OPEC have ever held much in the way of moral authority.

In the long run, the picture is more hopeful. Once things settle down and Turkey assumes a calming leadership role while the Levantine and Mesopotamian Shia zones exert balancing and moderating influence, the Muslim world could look more like Tunisia than Libya if there is anything left of it.

Turkey is positioned to gain in historic ways from the Sunni Spring. Since at least 1995, it has transitioned itself from being a bastion of secularism to a bastion of Islamism. It is perfectly in step with the political and social mood of the region. Unlike any other power in the region, it also has a tradition of moderation, social justice, and good, representative governance. Every inch of ground that Iran cedes in the realms of influence in Syria and leadership of pan-Islamism is ground that Turkey can occupy. The Gulf States, no matter how much money they have to influence candidates and promote their religious ideology, will not offer the sort of leadership that Syria, Egypt, or the North African states are looking for. These states do not look to Saudi Arabia, Qatar, or the Gulf in general, as a model for their societies or their political structures. While Turkey may not be as resource-rich as Saudi Arabia, neither is it resource cursed. It has ample human resources to dedicate to capacity-building and development in the Arab world and it will not hesitate to expand its prestige and influence in the region by using them.[60]

As Iran declines in regional influence and leadership of the resistance ideology against Israel and the West, Turkey may assume something of these roles. The latter, it will take on, however, to a far less severe degree. Turkey will not bluster about wiping Israel off the map and it will not espouse the notion of a war with the West. Turkey is a bridge-builder, in its self-understanding, between Islam and the West. That said, it is possible that the Turks might see a reduced need to remain a NATO member if their

---

[60] Goldman, *How Civilizations Die*, 67.

calculus leads them to believe that they can play a deeper and larger role in the Islamic world without being one.

Turkey is not without its problems. The Kurds of Turkey's undeveloped East are having at least twice the number of children as its developed West.[61] President Tayyip Erdogan has even predicted national destruction by 2038 "when the cost of supporting the bulge-generation of Turkish retirees will bankrupt the national Treasury, and when Kurdish speakers will threaten to outnumber Turks in Anatolia."[62] Only against the background of such civilizational angst, Goldman argues, might we make sense of Erdogan's bizarre 2008 outburst in Germany when he told 20,000 Turks in that country that assimilation into German culture was "a crime against humanity."

Turkey is well aware that it has an historic opportunity to form what Huntington calls a core state for Sunni Islamic Civilization. Huntington saw the divide between Sunni and Shia as being sub-civilizational.[63] Iran interacted with multiple states and non-state actors in the region as it funded Hamas, worked closely with states like Omar Bashir's Sudan, and consolidated its client relationship with Syria. According to Vali Nasr, Khomeini's is a "strategy of focusing attention on the United States and Israel to divert attention from the sectarian divide."[64] Thus a pan-Islamic unity is generated by the creation of external enemies that overcome the internal differences within Islam. Since the fall of Saddam Hussein, this trend has reversed itself. Since then, Iran has been forced into an ever more antagonistic position with the Sunni world, successes like Hezbollah's war against Israel notwithstanding. While Iranian rhetoric holds a revival of Ottoman Imperialism, as it calls a consolidated Turkish leadership of the region, to be its greatest strategic threat, over the long term, a weakened Iran could fall into a moderate and inclusive Turkish-led Muslim order that just as Iraq and Lebanon could. There exists no ideology of civilizational separation of Sunni and Shia on either side of that divide. Meanwhile, memories of Arab

---

[61] Ibid., 56.
[62] Ibid., 53.
[63] Huntington, *Clash of Civilizations*, 174-179.
[64] Nasr, *Shia Revival*, 226.

racial superiority ideology, as well as of Ottoman Imperial misrule are all but faded. Turkey has a momentous opportunity to form the core of a newly Islamist but also newly democratic Middle East. As a core state, it could be a great force for peace and stability.[65]

Summary and Conclusions

Long before any of these possibilities is realized, Syria is going to fall. The question is what comes after and what happens to the minorities. The question has profound implications for Lebanon and Iraq and even threatens the possibility of a re-drawing of the region's borders. The abortive French mandate-era notion of independence to an Alawite State along the coast north of Lebanon could come into belated (though perhaps only *de facto*) existence.[66] Many Syrian Christians would prefer citizenship in such a state to life in a resolutely Sunni Syria.[67] This state might or might not eventually join with Lebanon. Lebanon and the *de facto* Alawite state could find they have less in common with their Sunni neighbors and more in common with Israel. Iran will be marginalized in the region and already is finding its power and influence in Egypt and Syria highly curtailed and limited. It too may find common cause with Israel. Just as the US has many excellent strategic reasons to want to weaken Iran, it has several good reasons to not weaken it too much. Iran's nuclear ambitions are not merely to balance against the West or Israel. They are to balance against the Sunni hegemony of the Islamic world. As Huntington noted, Pakistan's bomb must be understood in light of Iran as well as India.[68]

The fall of Asad's Syria and possible war with Iran may well be the most pressing items on the agenda of the world. These events are as fraught with unforeseeable possible calamity as anything since the Cold War. It is an odd way to go into a strategic pivot away from the Middle East and toward East

---

[65] Huntington, *Clash of Civilizations*, 178.
[66] Abby Arganese, "Prospects for an Alawite State," on The Buzz (Blog of The National Interest), entry posted August 4, 2012, http://nationalinterest.org/blog/the-buzz/prospects-alawite-state-7286 (accessed August 15, 2012).
[67] Ibid.
[68] Huntington, *Clash of Civilizations*, 317.

Asia. There may come a time when America's Middle East policy can run on off-shore balancing and diplomacy. A realistic appraisal of the Arab Spring reminds us how far distant that goal remains.

BIBLIOGRAPHY

Akram, Fares and Isabel Kershner. "Hamas Premier Visits Iran in Sign of Strong Relations." *The New York Times*, 10 February 2012, http://www.nytimes.com/2012/02/11/world/middleeast/hamas-premier-ismail-haniya-visits-iran.html (accessed August 15, 2012).

Alawi, Ayyad. *The Crisis of Islamic Civilization*. Hartford, CT: Yale University Press, 2009.

Amos, Deborah. *Eclipse of the Sunnis: Power, Exile, and Upheaval in the Middle East*. New York, NY: PublicAffairs, 2010.

Armstrong, Karen. *Islam: A Short History*. New York: Modern Library, 2002.

Bajoria, Jayshree. "Demographics of Arab Protests: An Interview with Ragui Assaad, Professor, Humphrey School of Public Affairs, University of Minnesota." *Council on Foreign Relations*, February 14, 2011, http://www.cfr.org/egypt/demographics-arab-protests/p24096 (accessed May 12, 2012).

Black, Ian. "Fear of a Shia Full Moon." *The Guardian*, 26 January 2007, http://www.guardian.co.uk/world/2007/jan/26/worlddispatch.ianblack (accessed July 10, 2012).

Black, Ian. "The Libyan Islamic Fighting Group: From al-Qaida to the Arab Spring." *The Guardian*, 5 September 2011, http://www.guardian.co.uk/world/2011/sep/05/libyan-islamic-fighting-group-leaders (accessed September 5, 2011).

Buzz Blog, The. http://nationalinterest.org/blog/the-buzz/ (accessed August 15, 2012).

Center for Islam and Science. "Sayyid Jamal al-Din Muhammad." http://www.cis-ca.org/voices/a/afghni.htm (accessed August 15, 2012).

Cook, Michael. *Forbidding Wrong in Islam: An Introduction*. New York, NY: Cambridge University Press, 2003.

Dawisha, Adeed. "Requiem for Arab Nationalism." *Middle East Quarterly* 10, no. 1 (Winter 2003).

Demant, Peter. *Islam vs. Islamism: The Dilemma of the Muslim World*. Westport, CT: Praeger, 2006.

Fromkin, David. *Peace to End All Peace*. New York, NY: Henry Holt, 1989.

Gause III, F. Gregory. "Don't Just Do Something, Stand There!" *Foreign Policy*. December 21, 2011, http://www.foreignpolicy.com/articles/2011/12/21/america_arab_spring_do_nothing?page=full (accessed October 10, 2012).

Gettleman, Jeffrey. "As Syria War Roils, Unrest Among Sects Hits Turkey." *The New York Times*, 4 August 2012, http://www.nytimes.com/2012/08/05/world/middleeast/turkish-alawites-fear-spillover-of-violence-from-syria.html?pagewanted=1&src=recg (accessed August 15, 2012).

Goldman, David P. *How Civilizations Die: And Why Islam Is Dying Too*. Washington, DC: Regnery, 2011.

Haykel, Bernard. "On the Nature of Salafi thought and Action: Appendix al-Qaeda's Creed and Path." In *Global Salafism: Islam's New Religious Movement*, edited by Roel Meijer. New York, NY: Columbia University Press, 2009.

Howard, Michael. "America and the World." Lecture, Annual Lewin Lecture at Washington University, St. Louis, MO, April 5, 1984.

International Crisis Group. "Tentative Jihad: Syria's Fundamentalist Opposition." *Middle East Report N°131*, October 12, 2012, http://www.crisisgroup.org/en/regions/middle-east-north-africa/egypt-syria-lebanon/syria/131-tentative-jihad-syrias-fundamentalist-opposition.aspx (accessed October 15, 2012).

Kerr, Malcolm H. *The Arab Cold War*. New York, NY: Oxford University Press, 1971.

Lawrence, T.E. *Seven Pillars of Wisdom: A Triumph*. New York, NY: Anchor Books, 1991.

Lewis, Bernard. *Islam in History: Ideas, Men, and Events in the Middle East*. New York, NY: Library Press, 1973.

Mishra, Pankaj. "In 'Deep State' of Pakistan, an Unplanned Revolution Is Now Rewriting the Future." *The Jakarta Globe*, April 24, 2012, http://www.thejakartaglobe.com/opinion/in-deep-state-of-pakistan-an-unplanned-revolution-is-now-rewriting-the-future/513529 (accessed June 3, 2012).

Mitchell, Richard P. *The Society of the Muslim Brothers*. New York, NY: Oxford University Press, 1969.

Mneimneh, Hassan. "The "Turkish Model" in Arab Islamism: Rejection or Emulation?" The Hudson Institute's Center on Islam, Democracy, and the Future of the Muslim World, April 22, 2011, http://www.currenttrends.org/research/detail/the-turkish-model-in-arab-islamism-rejection-or-emulation (accessed September 1, 2012).

Mneimneh, Hassan. "The Spring of a New Political Salafism?" Current Trends in Islamist Ideology, vol.12 (October 2011), http://www.currenttrends.org/research/detail/the-spring-of-a-new-political-salafism (accessed July 12, 2012).

Nasr, Vali. *The Shia Revival: How Conflicts in Islam Will Shape the Future*. New York, NY: Norton, 2006.

Oren, Michael B. *Power, Faith, and Fantasy: America in the Middle East 1776 to the Present*. New York, NY: Norton, 2007.

Pelham, Nicholas. *A New Muslim Order: The Shia and the Middle East Sectarian Crisis*. New York: NY, I.B. Tauris, 2008.

Pieper, Joseph. *Leisure as the Basis of Culture*, trans. Gerald Marsbury. South Bend, IN: St. Augustine's Press 1998.

Pollack, Kenneth M. "America's Second Chance and the Arab Spring." *Foreign Policy,* December 5, 2011, http://www.foreignpolicy.com/articles/2011/12/05/americas_second_chance?page=0,2 (accessed October 10, 2012).

Pollack, Kenneth. *Arabs at War.* Omaha, NE: University of Nebraska Press, 2002.

Rubin, Alissa J. "Retiring U.S. Envoy to Afghanistan Exhorts Leaders to Heed Lessons of Past." *The New York Times*, 28 July 2012, http://www.nytimes.com/2012/07/29/world/asia/ambassador-crocker-sees-fraught-foreign-landscape-ahead.html?pagewanted=all (accessed August 15, 2012).

Schmitt, Carl. *Political Theology: Four Chapters on the Concept of Sovereignty*, trans. George Schwab. Chicago, IL: The University of Chicago Press, 1985.

Sindawi, Khalid. "Jordan's Encounter with Shi'ism." *Current Trends in Islamist Ideology*, vol. 8 (June 2009), http://www.currenttrends.org/research/detail/jordans-encounter-with-shiism (accessed July 12, 2012).

Sindawi, Khalid. "The Shiite Turn in Syria." *Current Trends in Islamist Ideology*, vol. 10 (August 2010), http://www.currenttrends.org/research/detail/jordans-encounter-with-shiism (accessed July 9, 2012).

Steinberg, Guido. "Jihadi Salafism and the Shi'is: Remarks about the Intellectual Roots of anti-Shi'ism." In *Global Salafism: Islam's New Religious Movement*, edited by Roel Meijer. New York, NY: Columbia University Press, 2009.

Stewart, Rory. *The Places In Between.* London, UK: Picador, 2004

Zakaria, Fareed. *The Future of Freedom.* New York, NY: Norton, 2003.